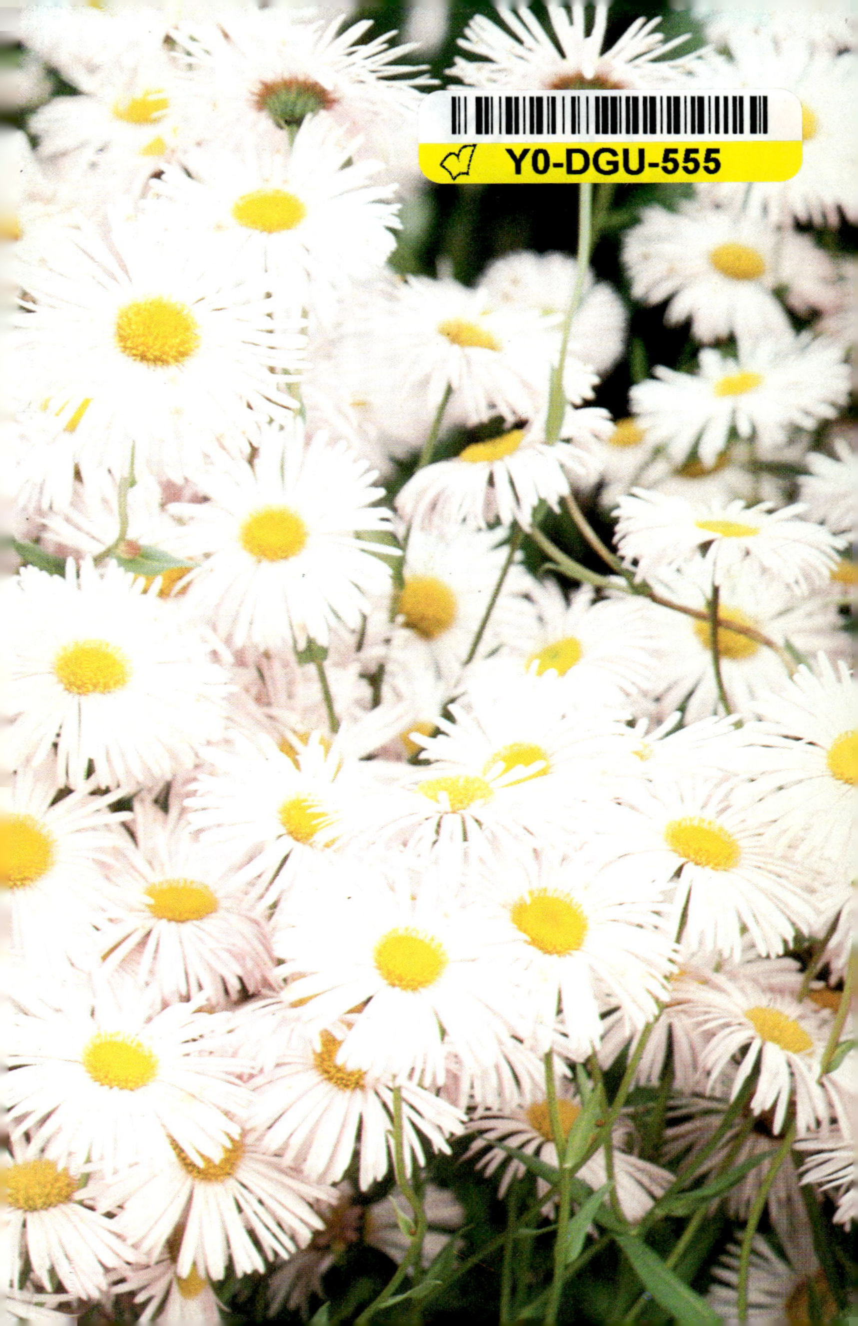

# Only Believe in Him

by AUDREY McDANIEL

The C. R. Gibson Co. Norwalk, Connecticut

*. . . in the morning will I direct my prayer unto thee, and will look up.*

PSALM 5:3

PHOTO CREDITS

Courtesy of the state of Vermont — Cover, P.10;
Penny Pederson — endpapers; Leonard Bacon — p.6, p.19;
Steve Mack — p.15, p.22; Elizabeth P. Welsh — p.27.

Copyright © MCMLXXVII by
The C. R. Gibson Company, Norwalk, Connecticut
All rights reserved
Printed in the United States of America
ISBN: 0-8378-2018-9

I love the Lord because he hath heard my supplications.

Because he hath inclined his ear unto me, therefore will I call upon him as long as I live.

In God nothing is hopeless, because He will always give ear to His children.

He will extend manifold benefits, soothe our troubled hearts, with a Love as reassuring as a rainbow's everlasting Promise.

There is nothing to fear when the Lord is on our side. There is no burden that cannot be cast out of our lives, when we lift it up to God in faith.

He raiseth the poor, and lifteth the needy and He causeth our cup to runneth over with Love when we silently commune with Him.

Therefore, with a cheerful heart shall we walk before the Lord in the land of the living.

*Only believe in Him.*


I love Him because He heard my plea
For the Gift of Christ that set me free
So now in a moment of deep despair
I have only to speak to God in prayer
Knowing His Love will come to me
Comfort and guide me eternally.

*Yea, I will rejoice over them to do them good, and I will plant them in this land assuredly with my whole heart and with my whole soul.*

JEREMIAH 32:41

Earthly love may fail us, and even break our spirit, but the Love of God is constant.

There is no peace amidst all the pleasures life has to offer until God is part of our every plan.

Earthly joys are a meager preview of the wonderful Love of God.

Once we have known His Love, no other love can suffice.

He offers this sacred affection so generously that we do not have to wonder if He cares . . . we have only to turn to Him, and the happiness that overtakes us bespeaks His true devotion.

Only my Father's Love will do
No other love is quite so true
Freely He showers affection on me
Caring and comforting, setting me free
Making me know I am really His Own
The most precious Love 'neath Heaven's Throne.

*And the work of righteousness shall be peace; and the effect of righteousness quietness and assurance for ever.*

Isaiah 32:17

Life finds new meaning when we endeavor to walk the righteous path with God.

In this beautiful association, the heart finds peace . . . happiness and security . . . full measure pressed down.

God's Love affords a calming quietness . . . a Love of such immensity that it can blend our human spirit with divine spirit for celestial purpose.

*Only believe in Him.*

<br>

O Father I'm not worthy to look up
And yet I raise my seeking eyes to Thee
For Thou art qualities beyond compare
Beautiful, celestial and rare
E'en in my feeble state of mind
Thou art so loving and so kind
Resentment, fears seem set aside
In peace and joy we now abide
O precious Father never go
There is such comfort in this glow
Abide in me forevermore
That only Thee may I adore.

*. . . they shall obtain joy and gladness, and sorrow and sighing shall flee away.*

Isaiah 35:10

When the Spirit of God's Love abideth in us, we shall go forth in joy.

He shall lead us in paths of peace, and our works shall be to His honor and glory.

Each life can make a beautiful contribution to God . . . if we will listen to His Words of Wisdom and be guided by His lovingkindness.

In this sacred relationship, our lives shall be transformed, for the nearness of Him brings its own changing powers.

Life finds new meaning . . . hearts are motivated by love and beautiful things of the soul are then expressed.

> O teach me to walk in Thy sacred way
> Instill in me faith as I kneel to pray
> Not for the things of my heart alone
> But for all children 'neath Thy Throne
> Guiding my feet lest I slip or stray
> Bless me O Father each hour of the day.

*And I will give them an heart to know me, that I am the Lord: and they shall be my people, and I will be their God: for they shall return unto me with their whole heart.*

JEREMIAH 24:7

We acquire only a meager percentage of life's happiness when we walk outside the realms of God's great Love.

Only in the shadow of His Wings can we know true joy. In His beautiful example . . . a worthwhile way that permeates our very souls . . . can peace of heart be found.

Loving others, as He loves us, is another milestone on the pathway that leads to satisfying happiness.

In His dear Presence, our hearts are motivated to things of the spirit . . . things eternal and everlasting.

*Only believe in Him.*

The precious Love I know with Thee
Is wonderful dear God to me
It fills my heart with sheer delight
Thou art my strength, my hope, my light
It teaches me to offer Love
To work for only Thee above
It takes away the wrongs I do
And brings me to the heart of You.

*Every word of God is pure: he is a shield unto them that put their trust in him.*

Proverbs 30:5

Things of this earth are transient . . . but the words of our heavenly Father endure forever.

They are a lamp unto our feet to guide us eternally. Our lives find peace and fulfillment when we seek to let these words flow through us. What enters our hearts does not defile us but what comes out of our hearts may destroy or bless.

There is an endless mission to be done daily in life. All around us, struggling lives are in need of a word of hope and love from God's vast storehouse of bountiful blessings.

Teach me my Father Thy Words to say
Seeking Thy Will, not mine as I pray
Give me a daily task to do
Use my whole heart in service for You.

*. . . ye shall go out with joy, and be led forth with peace: the mountains and the hills shall break forth before you into singing, and all the trees of the field shall clap their hands.*

Isaiah 55:12

This is the happiness the righteous may enjoy, when they relinquish their ways and their thoughts for the ways of the Lord.

Each day brings new opportunities to witness for God. It is His Will that others be blessed for His Sake, through our affection, our faith.

This is the Way to Happiness . . . as we strive to reflect the beautiful example of Christ. . . that others may find peace, and God.

Then shall the world before us break forth with singing . . . and the trees clap their hands.

Please Father touch my lips with peace
That some seeking heart find release
Through some small word or quiet prayer
I offer to Thee for their care
Then may a song ring in their heart
Filled with Thy comfort to ne'er depart.

*... If a man love me, he will keep my words: and my Father will love him, and we will come unto him, and make our abode with him.*

JOHN 14:23

Jesus did everything possible to assure us of our Father's Love. He sponsored us in His final hour, not praying for His own concern but beseeching God to have Faith in us.

He stands always at the door of our hearts asking that we lift the latch that He may enter.

He is laden with all good gifts for us, and He offers to come into our lives, that our joy may be made full.

I've felt Him take my hand in prayer
I've known His Love beyond compare
I've sought Him early on the way
And had Him stay with me all day
I've seen the storm clouds disappear
When Love like this was ever near
I've longed to walk close by His Side
In peace so sweet to e'er abide.

*... that we may lead a quiet and peaceable life ...*

1 Timothy 2:2

We, ourselves, can never solve the problems of this life relying on our own judgment . . . but we can always call on the resources of God's Intelligence and Love to handle these issues.

There is absolute security leaning on the Arm of God.

He tells us before we call, He will answer . . . and while we are yet speaking, He will hear.

He who promised will be faithful.

His Love is as sweet as a dew kissed Rose . . . and His peace like a sacred prayer.

*Only believe in Him.*

In a garden filled with roses<br>
Stood a Saviour sweetly dear<br>
And it seemed a bit of heaven<br>
With this precious Friend so near<br>
His tender Words of sacred Love<br>
Fell on the blossomed air<br>
And suddenly the tiny birds<br>
Sang like a lilting prayer<br>
In every nook and crevice<br>
The garden whispered Love<br>
For Christ was teaching that sweet day<br>
The way to heaven above.

*. . . and the desert shall rejoice, and blossom as the rose . . .*

Isaiah 35:1

God, in His infinite Love, placed us in a garden spot of beauty . . . that only He could design.

Midst the tiny blossoms that enhance the earth . . . the soft rain that appeareth at His command . . . deeds of kindness exchanged by friends on the highway of life, that warm the heart . . . all these, and more, are the works of a wonderful Father.

May our spoken words and silent thoughts ever preserve this loveliness.

May our prayerful hearts convey to God our appreciation for the wonders of His Love.

In the heart of a rose
Filled with morning dew
A lesson in faith was shining through
It turned to God for its only keep
In quiet repose it folded in sleep
Knowing at morning's early light
Its petals would open a heavenly sight
Its fragrance would fill the dawning air
Reflecting its Father's Love and Care.

*He hath made every thing beautiful in his time: . . .*

ECCLESIASTES 3:11

The plan of God is perfection and beauty. Each step of the way ordained to give us security and serenity.

Man's own plan becomes disrupted and full of chaos but the plan of God is always in order.

We cannot project our own lives and find peace of soul but we can turn to God for His peace that passeth all understanding.

No problem is too big for Him to solve, no blessing too impossible to receive . . . trusting Him.

When we place the cares of our lives into God's Arms of Protection . . . the Answer will always be a right one.

Help me the struggle now to end
For I have Thee as a Saviour and Friend
Breathe on me Lord Thy precious care
Wideness of mercy, hope in despair.

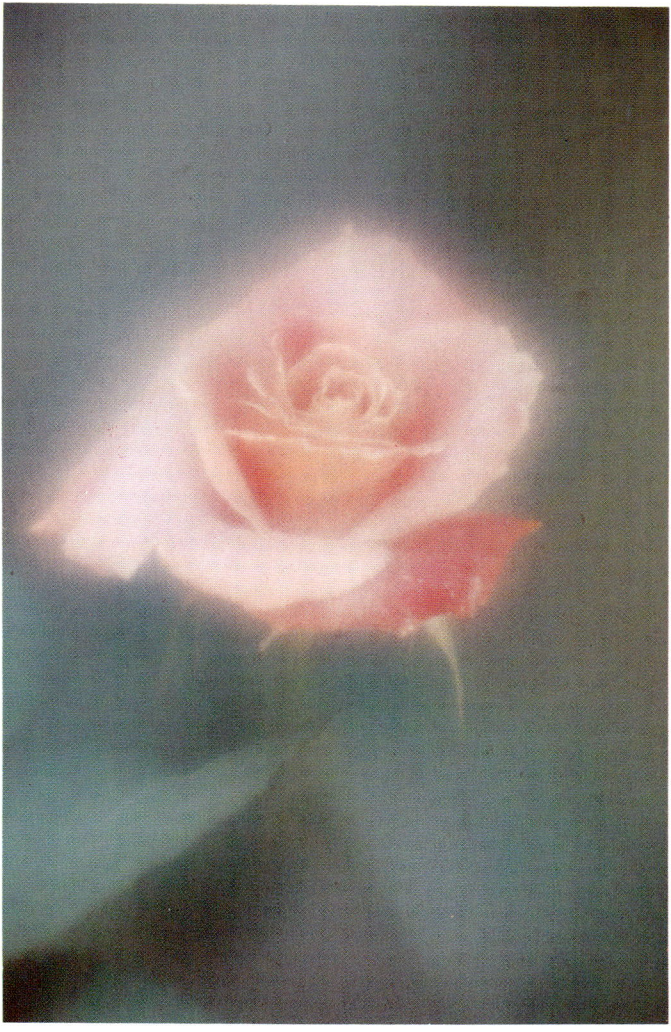

*I, even I, am the Lord; and beside me there is no saviour.*

Isaiah 43:11

Jesus was the true example of Perfect Love.

He saw all mankind through the eyes of love. When He taught His disciples at the Galilee Hill . . . Love was His Theme.

In the beautiful 17th Chapter of John . . . He prayed lovingly to His Father for us. "I pray for them . . . for they were thine . . . and they now are mine."

His is a Love that has pierced through all the ages of time as the only solution to human problems.

It is the Alpha and Omega of our existence . . . for God is Love.

Then the way to happiness for us . . . is the way of love.

*Only believe in Him.*

We met on the Galilee Hill one day
We met in prayer and I heard Christ say
Give unto others all the way
The same as I'm teaching thee here today
Seeking no praise or earthly reward
For riches in heaven for thee shall be stored
Then serve the less fortunate in need of love
And I will watch over thee from above.

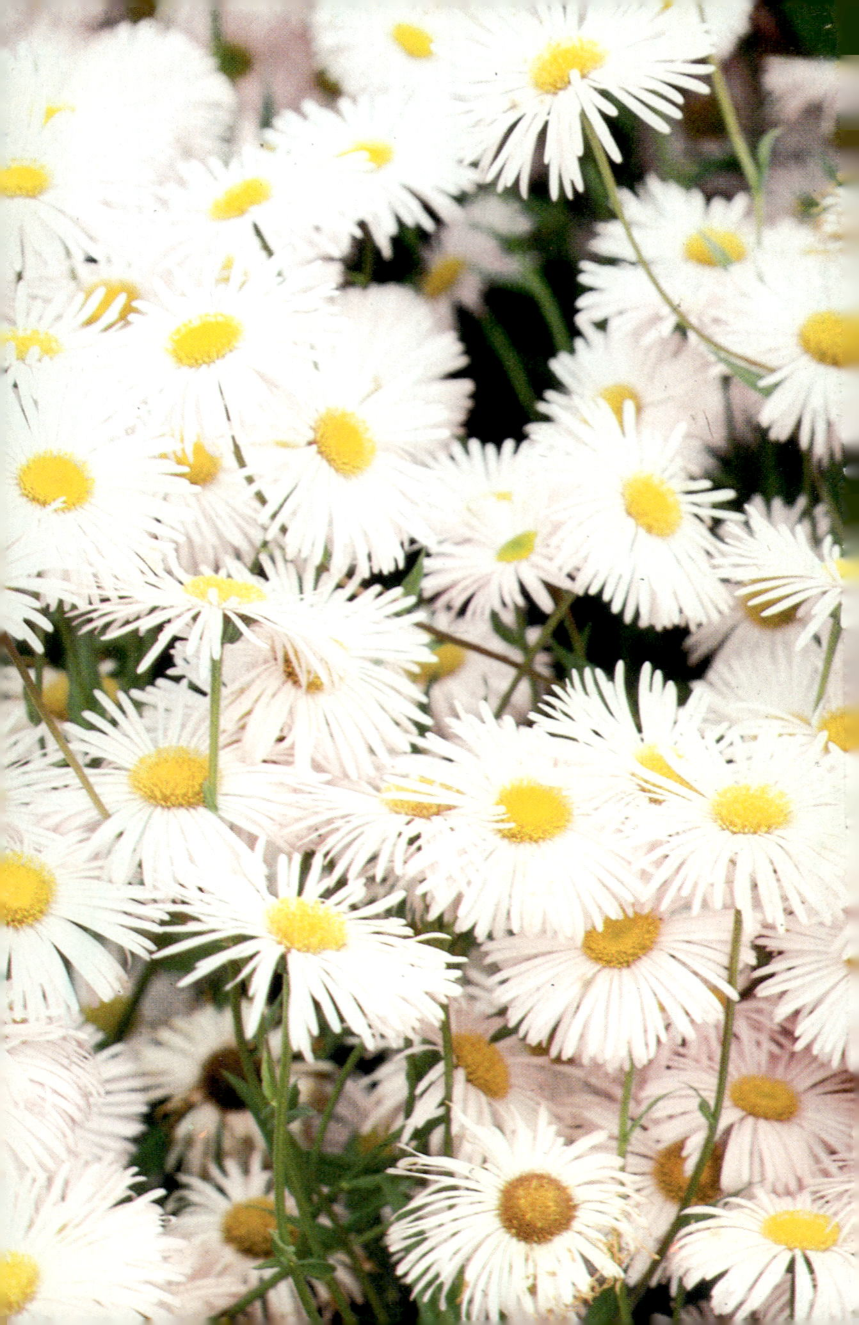